James Moffatt

A brief history of the conflict between the United States and Spain

Spain

1898

James Moffatt

A brief history of the conflict between the United States and Spain
1898

ISBN/EAN: 9783337231927

Printed in Europe, USA, Canada, Australia, Japan

Cover: Foto ©ninafisch / pixelio.de

More available books at **www.hansebooks.com**

A

BRIEF HISTORY

Of the Conflict Between

THE UNITED STATES
AND SPAIN

1898

WITH A FEW FINE ENGRAVINGS

By

JAMES STANLEY MOFFATT

Age Twelve Years

WEST PALM BEACH, FLORIDA

1899
HILL PRINTING CO
EUSTIS, FLA

JAMES STANLEY MOFFATT.

PREFACE.

———

At the outbreak of the Spanish-American War I thought of gathering all the facts relative to the conflict. Having recorded each incident as soon as it was confirmed, I am able to present to the public comparatively accurate, though brief, accounts of all the engagements and important movements of the war.

As I am only twelve years of age and this is my first attempt to write a book of any kind, no one need expect lengthy comments or flowery language in this little book. But those who wish a plain, convenient record of all the events of the war will find herein satisfactory work.

I trust that my simple efforts will be appreciated by all who read these pages.

JAMES STANLEY MOFFATT.

WEST PALM BEACH, FLA., Jan. 2, 1899.

THE SPANISH-AMERICAN WAR.

IN EIGHTEEN HUNDRED AND NINE-ty-five the Cubans rebelled against Spain, their mother country, and formed a Government of their own, which they called a Republic, electing Salvador Cisneros President and Bartolome Masso Vice-President.

Spain tried to put down the rebellion and sent, in all, between two and three hundred thousand soldiers to the island, and ever since the Spanish soldiers have been carrying on a most cruel warfare, murdering men, women and children, which was contrary to the modern rules of warfare between civilized nations and a violation of international law. This caused all civilized nations to sympathize with Cuba's oppressed people, though none of them recognized her Government.

The Spanish Government in Spain became careless and let her officials in Cuba do as they pleased. They killed and imprisoned a number of American citizens. This made the people of the United States very angry with Spain, and the Government sent the battleship Maine to Ha-

vana, the capital of Cuba, to protect her citizens
and *General Lee, who was Consul-General there.

As was customary, one of the harbor pilot
boats piloted the Maine into the harbor and left

MARIA CHRISTINA.

her at a Government buoy.   A few days later she
was moved from her safe anchorage to another

*General Lee, who was a Confederate soldier in the Civil
War, was at this time United States Consul-General at Havana.
He showed great bravery while among the cruel Spaniards, for
which the Government gave him the rank of Major-General in
the army and put him in command of the Seventh Army Corps,
where he showed great ability in keeping his men and camps in
order. Recently he was appointed Governor of Havana Province, Cuba.

MAJOR GENERAL FITZHUGH LEE.

buoy. At 9:30 o'clock p. m. every one was startled by hearing a terrific explosion, which almost lifted the ship out of the water and tearing it to pieces, with the loss of 266 of our sailors, besides the loss of the ship, which is over $3,000,000. It was afterwards found to have been the explosion of a Government submarine mine, which was there to protect the harbor against a hostile ship in case of war, which was touched off by some Spaniard. The Spanish Government was responsible for the Maine disaster, and the United States Government demanded an indemnity, but Spain refused to grant it. This, of course, brought on a war between the two nations.

Hostilities were begun on the 21st of April by the United States gunboat Nashville capturing a Spanish merchantman off Key West, Fla. The prize was worth $10,000, but had to be returned to her owners, as a Declaration of War had not been made then.

War was formally declared on the 25th between the United States and Spain.

The first movement of the war was the blockade of Havana, Matanzas, Cardenas and several other Cuban seaports by the United States' North Atlantic Squadron.

Havana had some formidable defenses, such as the big forts of Morro Castle and Cabanas. In addition it was well protected by submarine mines.

BOMBARDMENT OF MATANZAS.

On the 27th of April the forts at Matanzas fired on the blockading squadron, and three of the warships, the monitor Puritan, the cruiser New York and the gunboat Cincinnati, returned the fire. A half-hour battle ensued. The American gunners made good shots and the forts were soon demolished and some of the guns dismounted. The Spanish gunners were poor shots and none of the American ships were hit.

BATTLE OF MANILA BAY.

The first great naval battle of the war was fought in Manila Bay, Luzon, one of the Philippine Islands.

The American fleet of three cruisers, the Olympia, the flagship, Baltimore and the Raleigh, two gunboats, the Boston and the Petrel, and one dispatch boat, the McCullough, under the command of Commodore (now Rear-Admiral) George Dewey of Vermont, left Hong Kong, China, the Asiatic Station, to capture or destroy the Spanish fleet spuposed to be at Manila. It arrived at Manila Bay on the night of April 30th. The fleet entered the harbor that night. The garrison at Corrigador Island, inside the harbor, saw some sparks from the McCullough's funnel and fired a few shots at the fleet, but not hitting them. Our ships kept on until opposite Cavite and waited until daybreak, when the Spanish fleet, consist-

Hugh McVoblurb.   Reina Christina,   Petrel.   Boston.   Olympia,   Raleigh.   Baltimore
                  Spanish Flagship.   U. S. Flagship.

THE BATTLE OF MANILLA BAY.
Copyright 1898.

ing of eleven war vessels, commanded by Admiral
Montejo, and all the forts, opened fire upon
America's five warships. Dewey ordered full
steam ahead and passed between the Spanish fleet
and forts, delivering terrific broadsides as they
circled around.

One of the Olympia's eight-inch shells entered the stern of Maria Christina, flagship, and
went half way through and exploded in the cen-
ter, blowing up the ship. All the rest of the fleet
were either sunk, burned or captured.

The forts and arsenal at Cavite were also
captured, and a great many stores with them.
The Spanish loss was three hundred killed and
four hundred wounded.

The cruiser Baltimore was the only American ship damaged at all, and that not enough to
speak of. A few men were wounded on her.

The total American loss was six men slightly
wounded.

Dewey could not capture the city of Manila
for want of land troops to occupy it. Afterwards
it was captured by troops under General Merritt.
(See page 40).

BATTLE OF CARDENAS.

On the 12th of May three United States war
vessels, the torpedo boat Winslow and the gunboats Wilmington and Hudson, steamed into
Cardenas Bay, Cuba, in search of Spanish war-

ships, which were hidden in the harbor. They
did not see them until suddenly the Spanish vessels
darted out and opened fire with the forts upon the
American fleet. At first the Spanish firing was
wild, but it soon became accurate and our vessels

ENSIGN WORTH BAGLEY.

were subjected to a severe fire, but answered
briskly with a hail of shells upon the ships and
forts. One of the Spanish ships was burned and
a warehouse on shore was burned by the fire
from the American fleet.

The American ships exposed themselves to the Spanish fire, and a shell from the forts entered the boiler-room of the Winslow, which was in command of Ensign Worth Bagley, and blew out her boiler. This rendered her helpless and she rolled around in the sea, but all that did not stop her firing. The Spaniards, seeing that she was helpless, concentrated their fire upon her. The gunboat Hudson, lying near by, ran along side and tried to throw a line to the Winslow, but failed the first time. Just then a shell burst among Ensign Bagley and six of his men, who were standing on the Winslow's deck, killing the Ensign and four of his men. After repeated trials the Hudson got a line to her and started off with her, when suddenly the line broke, leaving both vessels under the terrific fire of the Spaniards. There were only three men left to make the line fast this time, but it was finally done and the Winslow was towed to Key West, Florida.

Ensign Worth Bagley of North Carolina was the first American officer killed in the war. Had he lived he would likely have been promoted for his bravery in directing his vessel against the Spaniards.

BOMBARDMENT OF SAN JUAN, PORTO RICO.

Nine American warships on May 12th, under Rear-Admiral Sampson, bombarded the forts of San Juan, Porto Rico. His orders were to

After a drawing in HARPER's MAGAZINE. Copyright, 189-, [illegible], [illegible].

THE RESCUE OF THE "WINSLOW"

punish the forts, but not to capture them. For three hours the forts suffered a terrific fire from the American fleet, doing great damage. The Spanish loss was great.

Only two Americans were killed and several wounded.

BATTLE OF CIENFUGOS, CUBA.

The United States gunboats Nashville and Windom and the cruiser Marblehead steamed up Cienfugos harbor with orders to cut the telegraph cable between Havana and Santiago de Cuba.

The cable was cut by the crews of four small boats from the warships under a terrific fire. One man was killed and several were wounded. They had to go very close to the shore, which was lined with Spanish soldiers, and so were much exposed.

The Nashville and Marblehead completely demolished the Spanish batteries and set the city on fire. The Spanish loss was four hundred killed and wounded.

COLLISION OF THE COLUMBIA AND FOSCOLIA.

The United States cruiser Columbia, while cruising off Staten Island at the rate of eight knots an hour, Saturday, May 28th, in a dense fog, with lights out, in search of Spanish ships, collided with the British tramp steamer Foscolia. The Foscolia drove her bow into the Columbia twelve feet and broke it off, leaving a hole ten

feet wide and five feet below the water line in
the big cruiser.

At the time of the collision the Columbia's
water-tight bulkheads were open, but the crew
were so active that they were closed in time to
save the ship from sinking.

The Foscolia sank several hours later. The
skipper stayed by his sinking ship until she
plunged beneath the sea, and then he and all his
crew was rescued by the Columbia's boats. The
Columbia then steamed to New York, where she
went into the dry-dock for repairs.

SINKING OF THE MERRIMAC.

While Rear-Admiral Sampson, in command
of the United States fleet off Santiago, was trying
to plan a way to close the entrance to the harbor
so as to keep the Spanish fleet inside, Assistant
Naval-Constructor Richmond Pearson Hobson,
of the flagship New York, heard of it. He at
once went to Rear-Admiral Sampson and sug-
gested sinking the collier Merrimac, loaded with
coal, across the narrow channel. Admiral Sampson accepted the plan and asked for volunteers.
It seemed like certain death to venture in between those frowning forts, but over four thousand men offered themselves freely.

Seven men were selected, Lieutenant Hobson
in command, and Daniel Montague, George F.
Phillips, Osborn Diegnan, Francis Kelly, George

Charette and J. C. Murphy. Henry Van Cott and Randolph Clauson were very anxious to go, so stowed themselves away on the Merrimac. After she had started they came from their hiding places and were assigned by Lieutenant Hobson to positions as part of the crew.

REAR-ADMIRAL W. T. SAMPSON.

Just as day began to break the Merrimac, under full head of steam, started on her dangerous mission, but after going several hundred yards was recalled by signals from the flagship New York. Rear-Admiral Sampson saw that it

was getting too near day to go on with a prospect
of success. The next morning, June 3rd, the
Merrimac got started again, a little earlier than
before. She went ahead until very close under
the Spanish guns, when a picket boat discovered
her and fired several shots at her at very close
range, carrying away her rudder. These few
shots from the picket boat were followed by a
fierce fire from the forts on the hills. Every gun
that could be brought to bear upon the collier
was fired.

The Merrimac trembled under this terrific
fire, but Lieutenant Hobson did not notice any
of it ; he was bent upon getting the Merrimac to
the proper point. When there he tried to swing
her across the channel, but she did not answer
her helm, and he discovered for the first time the
loss of the rudder. He then ran her ahead until
near one side of the channel and dropped her
anchor, and as she swung around with the tide
he touched off the torpedoes, which had been pre-
pared, and sank her. The crew had launched a
raft and all got on it, Hobson being the last.
The plan was to try to work out of the harbor
with it, but that had to be abandoned, as there
was a head tide. And so they fell prisoners to
the Spanish Admiral, Cervera.

That day Admiral Cervera sent a long mes-
sage, under a flag of truce, out to Admiral Sampson, telling him that the crew of the Merrimac

and commander were not hurt and were under his care, and that he would treat them with the utmost kindness while they were in his charge.

Ensign Powell, who was in charge of a launch, waited outside of the channel, right under the guns of Morro Castle, to try to rescue Lieutenant Hobson and his men, until after sunrise, and until all hope of rescuing them was gone.

Lieutenant Hobson's deed was considered by many to be the most conspicuous piece of bravery that has been enacted for a long time. He has since been promoted to the rank of Naval Constructor.

BOMBARDMENT OF SANTIAGO DE CUBA.

On June 7th the American fleets, in command of Rear-Admiral Sampson and Commodore Schley, bombarded the forts at the entrance of Santiago de Cuba Bay for three hours, inflicting great damage upon them. The ships were drawn up in two lines. The first was led by Commodore Schley's flagship, the Brooklyn, followed by the Marblehead, Texas and Massachusetts, and turned westward all the time, keeping up a terrific fire on all the forts except Morro Castle, because Hobson and his men were in there. The second line was led by Admiral Sampson's flagship, the New York, with the New Orleans, Yankee, Iowa and Oregon following, and turned westward. The Vixen and Suwanee were on the left flank, watching the riflemen on shore, and the Dolphin and Porter did scouting duty on the right flank. During the bombardment the cruisers Reina Mercedes and Viscaya and the torpedo boat destroyer Furor, belonging to the Spaniards,

REAR-ADMIRAL W. S. SCHLEY.

were damaged somewhat. None of the American ships were hurt.

SOLDIERS LEAVE TAMPA.

The Fifth Army Corps, under Major-General Shafter, 16,000 strong, left Tampa, Florida, on the

9th of June to invade Cuba. They arrived at Santiago de Cuba a few days later and landed on the shore at Guantanamo, a few miles distant, where they were unloaded with their supplies.

ATTACK ON CAMP M'CALLA AT GUANTANAMO.

The transport Panther unloaded a battalion of marines, under Lieutenant-Colonel R. W. Huntington, on June 10th, at Guantanamo, where they formed a camp known as Camp McCalla. The next day they were attacked from the brush by the Spaniards and a hot fight ensued. For thirteen hours it raged. The American loss was four killed and one wounded. The Spanish loss is unknown, as they carried their dead and wounded away with them ; but it must have been considerable, for the next day, when the cruiser Marblehead landed reinforcements, the enemy retired and the ground that they had occupied was stained with blood.

MARINES ATTACK SPANISH CAMP.

June 14th the marines at Guantanamo, Cuba, marched over the hills to attack the Spanish camp. They got within two hundred yards before being discovered. The Spaniards at once opened fire upon them. The marines quickly moved in battle line, with the Cubans on the left flank. The bullets were whistling vigorously over their heads, but they settled down to their work as if at target practice and shot accurately. Very few Spaniards were in sight, but the puffs of smoke revealed their positions and helped the marines to do effective work. The Cubans did little.

For twenty minutes the air was alive with bullets, and it seemed that a bayonet charge would have to be made to dislodge the enemy, but in a few minutes the marines' fire got too hot for the Spanish soldiers and they began a hasty retreat.

The American forces advanced and burned the small camp and destroyed the only water supply within six or seven miles. They then returned to camp with a loss of one killed and several wounded. The Cuban loss was two killed and four wounded. The Spanish loss was forty killed and wounded.

TRIAL OF THE U. S. S. VESUVIUS.

At midnight on the 13th of June the dynamite cruiser Vesuvius, lying off Morro Castle at Santiago de Cuba, was ordered by Rear-Admiral Sampson to try her dynamite guns on the new fortifications on which the Spaniards were working. The battleship Oregon threw her great search-light on the spot where the Vesuvius was to fire. Then the Vesuvius aimed her big guns and fired three times. The Spanish soldiers got behind trees and brush, thinking that they could not be hit, but, to their surprise, they did not hear a shot until the two hundred pounds of guncotton from the Vesuvius exploded on the fortifications. The three shots tore up tons of earth. Rear-Admiral Sampson was very much pleased with the work of the Vesuvius. The rest of the night passed quietly.

ANNEXATION OF HAWAII.

On the 15th of June the House of Representatives passed the resolution to annex the Hawaiian Islands to the United States. The vote was 209 for and 90 against. It was afterwards signed by the President. The Hawaiians were overjoyed at the annexation, as that was what they were trying to have done for years.

SPANIARDS ROUTED AT SANTIAGO.

Friday, June 24th, one thousand dismounted cavalrymen, under command of Lieut.-Colonel Roosevelt and Colonel Wood, marched over the hills four miles from Santiago and attacked two thousand Spanish infantrymen, who were hidden in the woods, and completely routed them after an hour of very hard fighting. There were twelve Americans killed and about fifty wounded. The Spanish loss could not be obtained, because they carried off their dead and wounded, except twelve, who were found by the Americans after the battle. This was known as the battle of Las Guasimas.

LAS GUASIMAS
FRIDAY, JUNE 24TH, 1898
From notes taken in
the field by
CASPAR WHITNEY.

The topography is only approximately correct. The idea is to show merely the relative positions of front, roads, &c.

BATTLE OF SAN JUAN, PORTO RICO.

The United States auxiliary cruiser St. Paul, while holding the blockade on June 22d at San Juan, Porto Rico, was attacked by the Spanish third-class cruiser Isabel II, and the torpedo boat destroyer Terror. The Terror was behind the Isabel II until they were not far from the St. Paul. The Terror came out from behind the Isabel II and made a dash for the St. Paul. The St. Paul did not fire until the Terror was very near; then she let loose her whole broadside battery and then kept up a steady fire, which soon disabled the Terror, killing the chief engineer and one of the crew and wounding five others. The Terror was so badly damaged that small boats had to be lashed to her to keep her from sinking while the tug towed her into the harbor to be repaired.

The St. Paul was commanded by Captain Charles D. Sigsbee, formerly Captain of the ill-fated Maine. The St. Paul was not hurt.

THE CAMPAIGN BEFORE SANTIAGO DE CUBA.
CAPTURE OF SAN JUAN.

General Hawkins' brigade was ordered by Major-General Wheeler, on July 1st, to take San Juan block-house, one of the defenses of Santiago. The brigade was composed of the Rough Riders under Colonel Roosevelt, who showed great courage in this fight, and the Seventy-first New York

Volunteers, also some of the regular troops, all of whom were very brave and proved themselves to be worthy of the places which they had to fill.

As soon as they made the movement toward the block-house, which was on a hill, the Spaniards opened a terrific fire on them and kept it up until finally, as they dashed up the hill, the Spaniards became panic-stricken and fled.

CAPTURE OF EL CANEY.

On the same day Captain Allyn K. Capron, in command of a battery of artillery, bombarded the stone fort at El Caney, another stronghold, about four miles from San Juan and about the same distance from Santiago. During the bombardment he did not get an answering shot. But when Brigadier-Generals Lawton, Ludlow and Chaffee and their men started to take the fort by a charge the Spaniards poured a deadly fire down on them. They never halted, but rushed up to the heights and took possession.

When the sun went down on July 1st the American army was in possession of two of the most important positions overlooking the city of Santiago. They were won under tremendous disadvantages and by some of the most wonderful displays of heroism that has ever been witnessed.

The American loss was 253 killed (less than was killed on the Maine) and 462 wounded. The Spanish loss was over 2,000 killed and wounded.

From these two commanding positions (San Juan and El Caney) Major-General Shafter demanded the surrender of the city and army of Santiago de Cuba on July 3d, but the Spanish commander would not surrender.

In this campaign General Joe Wheeler, a

MAJOR-GENERAL SHAFTER.

Confederate General in the Civil War, showed great courage and bravery. At all times he led his men to battle in person, even though sick with fever. For his courage he received the thanks of the American people and Government.

DESTRUCTION OF CERVERA'S FLEET.

On the 3d of July the Spanish fleet, under
Admiral Cervera, consisting of the Christobal
Colon, flagship, Almirante Oquendo, Infanta
Maria Teresa and Viscaya and two torpedo boat
destroyers, Furor and Pluton, which had been

MAJOR-GENERAL WHEELER.

held in the harbor for six weeks by the combined
squadrons of Commodore (now Rear-Admiral)
W. S. Schley and Rear-Admiral W. T. Sampson,
made a dash around the stern of the sunken collier Merrimac and got outside the harbor. The

Brooklyn was the nearest to the entrance of the
harbor at the time, and so Commodore Schley attacked them all. They were heavier armored
than his ship was, but he went for them neverthe-

LIEUT.-COMMANDER WAINWRIGHT.

less. The other ships soon came up and took
part.

Lieutenant-Commander Richard Wainwright,
a former officer of the Maine, now of the little
auxiliary gunboat Gloucester, at first attacked
the big ships, but thinking of the two torpedo

boat destroyers he quickly turned on them both, and after a furious battle set them on fire and ran them ashore.

The Infanta Maria Teresa caught fire and ran ashore, then the Viscaya and Almirante Oquendo. The Christobal Colon was chased forty miles by the Brooklyn and the battleship Oregon ; then, seeing no chance for escape, the Colon surrendered. Had it not been for the Brooklyn, part of the Spanish fleet might have escaped.

Admiral Cervera and nearly all of his men were taken prisoners.

Some of the Spanish ships were not so badly damaged, and wrecking ships were sent there in hope of raising them and putting them in shape for the United States Navy. The Infanta Maria Teresa was raised by the plan of Lieut. Hobson after his exchange. After staying in the harbor of Guantanamo, Cuba, for repairs (as best as could be furnished) she started for Norfolk, Va., for docking and repairing. but had not gotten two hundred miles when a hurricane caught her thirty miles north of Waterburg's (or San Salvador) Island. Being very leaky and in such a heavy sea, she soon filled with water and had to be abandoned, but not until there was no possible hope of saving her. Then her crew of 114 got aboard the three tugs which were accompanying the

Maria Teresa and were carried safely to Charleston, S. C.

The Maria Teresa afterward washed ashore in two fathoms of water, one mile off Bird's Point, Cat Island, thirty miles from where she was abandoned by her crew, and was lost in spite of the great efforts made by the Government to save her.

Then Lieutenant Hobson began work on the Christobal Colon.

EXCHANGE OF LIEUT. HOBSON AND HIS MEN.

While the contending armies were lying in their trenches before Santiago de Cuba, Lieutenant Hobson, the hero of the Merrimac, and his men were exchanged. Fifteen Spaniards were given for the nine Americans.

While talking about the treatment, Lieutenant Hobson stated that the Spaniards treated him and his men very nicely. The first four days they were in Morro Castle they were moved to the city, where they remained up to the date of the exchange, July 6th.

SURRENDER OF SANTIAGO DE CUBA.

After refusing the several demands made by Major-General Shafter, General Toral, the Spanish commander, surrendered the Spanish army and city of Santiago de Cuba, July 17th, 1898, on the following terms:

"The United States agrees, with as little delay as possible, to transport all Spanish troops in

the district of Santiago de Cuba to the kingdom
of Spain.   The officers are to retain their side
arms, and officers and men to retain their personal
property.   The Spanish commander is authorized
to take the military archives belonging to the
surrendered district.   All the Spanish soldiers

LIEUTENANT R. P. HOBSON.

known as Volunteers, Morilizades and Guerrillas,
who wish to remain in Cuba, may do so under
parole during the present war, giving up arms.
The Spanish forces are to march out of Santiago
with the honors of war, depositing their arms at

COLONEL THEODORE ROOSEVELT.

a point mutually agreed upon, to await the disposition of the United States Government, it being understood that the United States Commissioners will recommend that the Spanish soldiers return to Spain with the arms they have so bravely defended. This leaves the question of the return of arms entirely in the hands of the Government.

"I invite attention to the fact that several thousand have surrendered, said by General Toral, to be about 12,000, against whom a shot has not been fired. The return to Spain of troops amounts to about s24,000, according to General Toral.

(Signed)   "W. R. SHAFTER,
                "Major-General U. S. Volunteers."

So, on the 17th of July, at 9 o'clock a. m., the Spanish forces under General Toral marched out of Santiago de Cuba and laid down their arms to the American forces. General Toral handed his sword to General Shafter, who soon returned it. General Shafter then took formal possession of the city. The yellow flag was hauled down and the stars and stripes raised over the Palace.

GERMAN CRUISER STOPPED.

While the German cruiser Irene was running the blockade on July 14th at Manila Bay, Philippine Islands, she was asked to stop by Rear-Admiral Dewey. On her refusal to do so, Rear-Admiral Dewey sent the gunboat McCullough after her. The McCullough fired a shot across her bow and the German cruiser hove to. Then the McCullough sent a boat to the Irene to see what she was doing. The German Admiral said that the Americans had no right to interfere with the German ships, but Dewey would not listen to him, as he was holding a strict blockade.

BATTLE OF NIPE.

By orders of Rear-Admiral Sampson, July 21st, four American warships, the cruiser Topeka and the gunboats Annapolis, Wasp and Leyden, under the command of Commodore Romey, entered the harbor of Nipe, on the North coast of the Province of Santiago de Cuba, and furiously bombarded the forts for about an hour. Three forts were silenced and the Spanish gunboat Jorge Juan was sunk. She was a three-masted one funnel ship of 960 tons displacement and 1,100 horsepower. She carried a crew of 146 and had 130 tons of coal. Her battery consisted of three 4.7-inch Hontoria guns, two 2.8-inch Krupp guns and two machine guns. Then the fleet took possession of the harbor. There was no American ship hurt nor any of their crews killed or hurt.

LANDING EFFECTED AT GUANICA.

On July 21st, Major-General Miles, Commander-in-Chief of the United States Army, left Guantanamo Bay, Cuba, for Porto Rico, and ar-

rived at Ponce, Porto Rico, July 25th. About
thirty marines from one of the ships landed and
attacked a small village, which was captured at
once and the Spanish flag hauled down and the

MAJOR-GENERAL MILES.

United States flag raised. This was the first one
floated over Porto Rican soil.

BATTLE OF MALATE.

The American outposts, numbering 508 men,
had been advancing and intrenching near Manila,
Philippine Islands, until Sunday, July 31st. This

being the Insurgents' feast day, they withdrew their left flank, leaving the American outposts exposed to the Spanish, who were intrenched three hundred yards distant. The Americans were only three-quarters of a mile from Fort Manila. That night about midnight, in an extremely heavy wind and rain storm, the Spaniards, numbering 4,000 men, attempted to capture the American outpost.

Fom our right flank came a volley of Mauser bullets; this was followed by a hail of steel from the trenches in front. It was a terrible moment for that little band (500) of the Utah and Pennsylvania boys in that hastily constructed trench only five hundred feet in length. There was no chance of escape, because Fort Manila was sweeping the road to Camp Dewey with its 8-inch guns to cut off the American retreat should they desire to. But the American men calmly waited the order to fire. Soon they heard the bugle sounding "Commence Firing!" Then it seemed as if a volcano had burst, and gun No. 1 of the Utah Battery sent a Schrapnel into the midst of the Spaniards. This was followed by the fire from the rest of the guns of Battery B.

The great jar of the guns of this battery broke the supports of the embasture and about two tons of earth fell on two of the guns. This silenced the fire for a few minutes, but the soldiers leaped over the earthworks and cleared the earth away in a short time and again trained the guns.

It was at this moment that Battery A opened fire. It was not an instant too late, for the whole Spanish force leaped over their works and were charging onto the Americans, covered by a deadly fire from the fort. They swarmed in from every side and got within fifty yards of the trench, when Battery K of the Third Artillery, armed with Krag-Jorgenson rifles, came rushing up and relieved half of the Tenth Pennsylvania. Then a steady stream of bullets was poured into the enemy. Whenever our 3-inch rifle shells burst among them our men could see the glisten-ing of the enemy's bayonets as they were falling back—the fire was too much for them. But for an hour and a half they held their ground about seventy-five yards from our trench, and during the bright flashes of lightning our men could see the enemy in large numbers trying to make a stand against our terrific fire. Though our men were outnumbered eight to one, they never lost an inch of ground.

The scene in our trench was one never to be forgotten. During the bright flashes of lightning our dead and wounded could be seen lying in blood-red water, while the tremendous roars of thunder drowned that of the cannon and the musketry. But neither the elements of heaven nor the destructive power of man could wring a cry of protest from the wounded; they handed over their cartridges and encouraged their comrades to fight. The Spaniards were finally defeated and beaten back into the city with a loss of 300 killed and about 1,000 wounded. Our loss was 8 killed and 40 wounded.

CRUISER SAN FRANCISCO HIT BY A SHELL.

While the United States cruiser San Francisco, the monitor Miantonomah and the auxiliary gunboat Sylvia were holding the blockade at Havana, Cuba, they were fired on from Morro Castle.

The big ships were at their regular stations, about six miles off shore, on August 11th, and that night steamed in, as usual, to about one mile off Morro Castle.

The night passed away quietly, but just as the first glimmer of dawn was breaking through the eastern skies, when, without an instant's warning, the lookout on the flagship San Francisco saw a puff of black smoke from Morro's big guns. Almost before he could realize what had happened 10 and 12-inch shells were screaming all around the ships.

The San Francisco signaled to the Sylvia to get out of range of the fort. The ships were not permitted to fire on the forts, and so they turned to get out of range. Just as the San Francisco swung around a 12-inch shell struck her stern and completely wrecked Commodore Howell's library and the after cabin.

He was on deck at the time and did not get hurt. The shell did no very serious damage, and in a short time its effects were completely removed.

BATTLE AND CAPTURE OF MANILA.

Rear-Admiral Dewey, in command of the United States fleet, and Major-General Merritt, in command of the land forces at Manila, Philippine Islands, on August 13th demanded an unconditional surrender of the city. The Captain-General of the city was given only one hour in which to decide. He refused. The American fleet advanced toward the city shortly after 8:35 o'clock a. m. in battle line, with flags at the masthead, the flagship Olympia leading the way, with the Raleigh and Petrel following. The Callao, under command of Lieutenant Tampan, crept close to the shore.

Perfect quiet prevailed in the lines on shore as the great ships cleared for action, silently advancing, and sometimes hidden by rain squalls. The Monterey, with the Charleston, Baltimore and Boston, formed the reserve.

At 9:35 a. m. a sudden cloud of smoke, green and white, completely hid the Olympia, and a shell screamed across two miles of turbulent water and burst near the Spanish fort at Malate, on the south side of Manila. Then the Raleigh and Petrel and the little Callao opened fire upon the shore end of the intrenchments. In the heavy rain it was difficult to judge the range, and at first our shells fell short, but the fire soon became

REAR-ADMIRAL DEWEY.

accurate and the shells rendered the fort untenable, while the guns of the Utah battery made excellent practice on the earthworks. The Spaniards replied feebly with a few shots.

GREENE ADVANCES.

Less than half an hour after the bombardment began General Greene decided that it was possible to advance. Thereupon six companies of the First Colorado Regiment leaped over their breastworks, dashed into the swamp and opened volley firing from the part shelter of the low hedges within three hundred yards of the Spanish lines. A few minutes more the remaining six companies of the same regiment moved along the seashore, somewhat hidden by a sand ridge formed by an inlet under the outworks of the fort, and at 11 o'clock they occupied the stronghold without loss. Lieutenant McCoy pulled down the Spanish flag and raised Old Glory, amid wild cheers of our men. Meanwhile the fleet, observing the movement of the troops along the shore, withheld its fire. The bombardment lasted an hour and a half.

An hour later General Greene and staff rode along the beach, still under heavy fire from the enemy, and directed the movements for an advance into Malate. The vicinity of the fort was uncomfortable on account of the number of sharpshooters in the buildings on both sides, two hundred yards distant. The forward movement was therefore hastened, and in a few minutes the outskirts of the suburb were well occupied and the sharp-shooters were driven away.

The American troops kept driving the Spaniards back until they were inside the walled city of Manila. Here, seeing that further resistance was useless, the Spanish commander surrendered to the American forces. Captain General Augustin escaped just before the surrender to Hong Kong China, in a German ship.

The American forces at once occupied the

MAJOR-GENERAL MERRITT.

city, with Major-General Merritt acting as Governor-General. The blockade was raised and the harbor opened to all ships, and the inhabitants resumed their usual business.

The American loss was 46 killed and 100

wounded.   The Spanish loss was about 100 killed
and 200 wounded.

THE PEACE PROTOCOL.

On the 12th of August, at 4:23 p. m., Secre-
tary Day of the United States and M. Cambon of

PRESIDENT M'KINLEY.

France for Spain, in the presence of President
McKinley, signed a protocol of peace.

THE LAST ENGAGEMENT OF THE WAR.

The last engagement of the war was the
bombardment of Manzanillo, Cuba. An Ameri-

can fleet, consisting of the gunboats Osceola, Hist
and Alvarado, appeared in front of the town and
demanded its surrender. The Spanish commander refused. Then the fleet commenced firing, and for half an hour it bombarded the city,
inflicting damage. In the afternoon they received the news of the protocol of peace and the
fleet steamed back to its regular station. There
was no damage done to the fleet nor was there
anyone hurt.

A SALUTE.

On the 20th of August the fleets of Rear-Ad-
mirals Sampson and Schley steamed up North
River, in New York harbor, to General Grant's
tomb and fired a salute to celebrate the early clos-
ing of the war and the home-coming of the vic-
tors.

SWORD PRESENTATION TO ADMIRAL DEWEY.

For Rear-Admiral Dewey's great daring and
skill in directing his ships against the Spanish in
Manila Bay, the United States Government had
a fine gold sword made and presented it to him
as a gift of the American people. It cost $3,000.
Beside all of this he was promoted to the rank of
Rear-Admiral.

THE BATTLESHIP OREGON.

The United States battleship Oregon, in command of Captain Clarke, had been doing duty in

the Pacific Ocean since her completion in 1893. On March 16th, 1898, she was ordered by the Government to proceed to the Atlantic Coast so as to take part in the approaching war, but when she got about one-third the way the war broke out. At once the Spanish warships set out for the Oregon, but they did not meet her, and did not want to very bad, because the big battleship could give them a warm reception.

Never meeting any opposition, the Oregon kept her course, only stopping to get coal and supplies. After 117 days she struck the United States at Jupiter, Florida, where she received orders from Washington and proceeded to New York.

The Oregon broke all records when she made this seventeen thousand mile voyage without stopping, and not needing five cents worth of repairing. Then going to Santiago de Cuba, she took an active part in the destruction of the Spanish fleet. For this great feat she was nicknamed the "Bulldog of the United States Navy."

On October 12th, 1898, she was ordered to retrace her voyage in company with the United States battleship Iowa, and then go 7,000 miles further to reinforce the Asiatic Squadron at Manila, Philippine Islands.

PORTO RICO OURS.

After several small battles and skirmishes on the island of Porto Rico, the American flag was raised over the Royal Palace at San Juan the capital of the Island) at noon on the 18th of October, 1898. The American troops then took formal possession of the Island.

THE COST OF THE WAR.

The cost of the war to the United States was as follows: For general expenses, $200,000,000; for the Philippine Islands, $20,000,000, and $2,-500,000 for the Maine disaster, which is not counted in the cost of the war, but was the real cause of it. Total cost, $222,500,000.

American loss in life was about 400 killed and 2,000 wounded in battle, and about 2,000 men died in camps. This does not include the 266 lives lost on the ill-fated United States battleship Maine.

SPAIN'S LOSSES.

The following are Spain's losses: Philippine Islands, $450,000,000; Cuba, $300,000,000; Porto Rico, $150,000,000; war expenditures, $125,000,000; commercial loss during the war, $20,000,000; twenty-one warships, $30,000,000; total, $1,075,000,000.

Spain's loss in life was about 2,500 killed and 3,000 wounded.

WHAT THE UNITED STATES GAINS.

The United States gains Porto Rico, area 3,500 square miles; Philippine Islands, area 114,-

326 square miles; Sulu, area 950 square miles; Guam, largest island of the Ladrones, area 120 square miles; Isle of Pines, area 1,214 square miles. Fifty-six Spanish merchant vessels were captured during the war.

This was the shortest, most honorable war the United States has ever had, but an expensive one.

THE FILIPINOS WAR.

ATTACK ON MANILA.

The long looked for trouble with the natives of the Philippine Islands was begun February 4, at 8:40 p. m., by the Filipinos crossing the lines of the Nebraska regiment's pickets at Santa Mosa, Luzon Island. After being challenged the Nebraska sentry fired into them, killing one and wounding another. These few shots seemed as a signal, and the whole rebel line on the north side of the Pasig river opened a fusilade. The American outposts returned the fire with such vigor that the Filipinos line was checked until reinforcements arrived, then a terrific fire was poured upon the Filipinos, but not doing much on account of the darkness. The fight had lasted an hour, when there was a lull over the whole battle-field, which lasted until 2:45 o'clock in the morning when it was resumed. Both kept up a terrific fire for about twenty minutes, then they waited for daylight, when the Americans advanced.

During the night, response in to Rear Admiral Dewey's signals, flashed across from Cavite, the United States cruiser Charleston and the gunboat Concord, stationed off Malabon, poured a deadly fire into the insurgents' trenches at Caloocan from their secondary batteries. After daylight the monitor Monadnone and the other vessels of Dewey's fleet shelled the Filipinos' right and left flank for several hours. By 10 o'clock the Americans had completely routed the rebels and advanced six miles, destroying many native huts and capturing several villages. The insurgents made a very determined stand at Paco church and convent. A body of Californians, stationed on a neighboring bridge, poured a terrific fire upon them, but not doing much; so, in the face of a terrific fire a few of them dashed into the church and poured coal oil on the walls and floor, set fire to the house and retired. Their loss was 4,000 killed; the American loss was 52 killed and 200 wounded.

SECOND ATTACK ON MANILA.

After being routed and driven six miles by the American troops, the insurgents renewed the desperate attack on Manila, but were routed and driven back ten miles with terrible slaughter. The Filipinos lost about 2,000 killed and 3,500 wounded and prisoners; the American loss was about 40 killed and 200 wounded.

TREATY OF PEACE.

"The treaty of peace negotiated between the commissioners of the United States and Spain at Paris, was ratified by the United States Senate February 6. The vote was 50 for and 27 against, or one more than the necessary two-thirds."

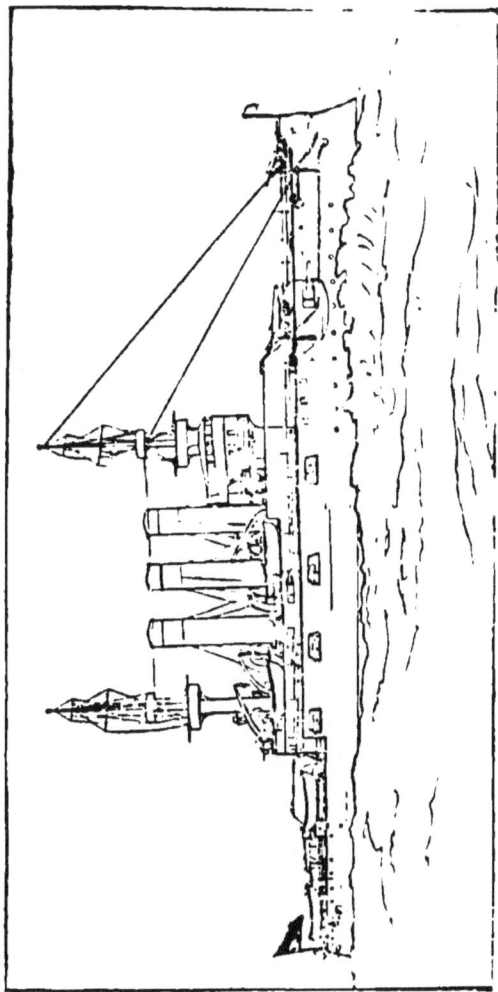

THE NEW "MAINE."

After a Drawing in *Harper's Weekly*. Copyright, 1896, by Harper & Brothers.

EMILIO AGUINALDO

www.ingramcontent.com/pod-product-compliance
Lightning Source LLC
Chambersburg PA
CBHW031806090426
42739CB00008B/1185